NOTES O HEALING AND CLARITY

POEMS BY

ERIN ELIZABETH WEHRENBERG

This is dedicated to anyone who is at any point in any process of healing; I'm with you.

All writings by Erin Elizabeth Wehrenberg.

Designed by Richard Wehrenberg, Jr.

———————————————

CONTENTS

"Indeed, no woman writer can write "too much"...No woman has ever written enough."

— *bell hooks*

Feel It and Know It

If you have to question

whether something
is or isn't

whether you
can or can't

whether things are
okay or not

you probably already know,
you are probably just seeking permission.

Impossible Heartbreak

There was life before.

And.

There will be life after.

Your Teachers Are All Around You

When I was twelve and
I took our newly adopted golden retriever for a walk,
I threw out all internalized bullshit assumptions
I was taught to hold
about everyone and everything because
he did not lift his leg to pee
when I expected him to.

You Got Into A Rut, Who Gives A Fuck?

Everything I feel is real.
All my experiences are real.
I trust myself.
I trust the process.
I can feel what is right and what is wrong.
I do not need to allow toxicity to flow into my life.
I am in control of my relationships, my choices.
I teach others how to treat me by what I will allow.
I am not a possession.
I am safe.
I love and accept myself.
There is nothing wrong with me.

Choice

"I can't do this anymore."
"Then don't do it."

How You Envision Yourself Is How You're Supposed To Be

When I was a little girl,
brown curls down to my butt
I saw myself, as an adult,

brown curls down to my breasts
so removed from who I was then,
but certain it was me.

In the woods, fruit and veggies in hand.
Always in skirts,
sun-kissed skin

A dog or two following me
as I explored the Earth as my truth
bare-footed and bare-boned.

Earth mother dreams
in the sunflower eyes
of a baby girl.

It Is Automatic For A Reason

Just as we must keep breathing when we experience physical pain
and inhale the deep air into our wound for relief,
we must keep breathing when we experience emotional pain.

Breathe in the infinite healing powers of the universe
and breathe life into these emotions coupled with pain.

There is no shame here; this is body mind working together to heal.
A process often looked down upon,
even though it is the most powerful.

Keep breathing.

Its power gives us life when we are unintentional,
feel how much power we unlock when it is intentional.

I Look At You and I Am Tired

It is impossible to hate all of you.
Of course I couldn't.

I do not feel shame when I have memories of tender moments,
I just know that those moments are not worth it anymore.
Not worth the trade off of pain.

You are the qualities that drew me in,
but you are also the qualities that made me leave.
And to that, I owe you nothing.

Honestly Honoring the Process of Past Pain

Cried for only 2 minutes on the car ride home today.
Began to speak aloud to myself,
taking turns with tears.

"There is too much betrayal
and ignored pain between us
for me to feel safe here again."

I imagined myself saying these things to you
and then feeling triumphant.

But I suppose waiting for the day you contact me again
doesn't really make me that triumphant...

Does it?

(actually, yes. yes it does make me triumphant. i thought about you
in a new way. a way that magnifies the truth. a way that is freeing and
to get to the final freedom takes time and takes baby steps. contrary
to what i was told, i will celebrate this because i am slowly shifting
to the place i know i am supposed to be and to ignore that process
is a disservice to myself. healing is a process that takes time. time
is a process that takes time. it's easy to forget, but time takes time.)

Lessons in Addictive Behaviors

For years,
I was so scared to control my own life
that I tried to control
the uncontrollable,
while also shuffling
through various addictive behaviors
in order to prove
false deep-rooted beliefs
about myself
to myself.

I'm sorry.

Social Media As A Distraction

Eventually
there
will
be
nothing
new
to
look
at.

DT3 Affirmations
(Or, "What Is Alive For You
Romantically and Sexually?")

It's okay.
I am safe.
It's okay how I feel.
I am cared about.

I Am Free To Love and Enjoy Life

Running from love, when things are easy,
because patterns of the past are not being matched,
is not protection.

It is self-destruction.

Brainwashed

How many women have I hated
unnecessarily, automatically, ruthlessly,
because of systems created by men
or because of actual men
in or out of my life
(silently) telling me to do so?

Too many.
Any number greater than zero
is too many.

Hey, Do You Have Any Lipstick?

If I rejected all the stereotypical feminine things I like or want to be
(just because they are rooted in patriarchy),
I am still letting patriarchy control me.

Just in a different way.

At The Expense of Whom?

Do artists really not understand
the power they hold
over the subjects they are mused by?

A choice to paintphotographwritedraw this
intensely
unbelievably
beautifully
complex human
in any way they want
to anyone and everyone.

Do you know this?
Can you feel the weight of this?

There is a cost
for "creating" irresponsibly.

You Do Not Have Permission To Use My Magical Body Against Me

"PMSing" is not a valid excuse for someone, anyone to
invalidate, dismiss, or name-call me
and my very real emotions.

This learned dismissal from others and of self shatters my heart and
removes me from the raw connection I have to the Earth
and the unfiltered wisdom that comes with my emotions.

I am not PMSing.
I am alive in alignment.

Shed

This same body contains
the continual intertwines
of all that I am
and all that I shall ever be.

An infinite process of becoming, shedding, and shifting
my energies and soul, tangibles and intangibles.

This is why I have never understood your question,
"What will you do for the rest of your life?"

I will become, shed, and shift
into new me's
but, somehow, I will still be me.

And so, to answer your question,
for the rest of my life,
I will become.

Dreams

In order to make room for your angel, you have to let go of the
protection.
In order to keep me from freezing over, I need you to swallow my
heart whole.

I do not need to change my mold to mesh into you.
I do not need to bend for you.
Close the door all the way.

"But plz know I miss you."

What's the difference between pretending it's real and it is real?
Still feels nice to roll your name off my tongue.

Peaches

Where are your toes and fingers?
The hands that stroked my hair so
and the voice that pressed laughter into my neck?
Your fingers curling into the small of my back
while my closed eyes breathed you in.
This October man.
Full of balance and fairness,
Especially with me.
"Thank you for letting me help you feel safe,"
The words meet my eardrums.
I smile as my words push open my teeth,
"There was no letting, no choice. Of course it was you."

I know you now, after this time together.
But of course it's deeper than that
I have always known you.
Our souls called
and packaged our lives.

And now, I ask again
where are your toes and fingers?

Irrational Numbers

I don't have time for your ego or mind games.
Don't you know how many times
humans have fucked up the deepest knowings
by trying to quantify the unquantifiable?
Processes we are meant to feel and know only through body wisdom.
Processes only the Earth unlocks.

I can feel the carefully calculated craft with which you define your life
because this feeling is met immediately with a clashing in my soul.

My love does not work this way.
My being is unquantifiable.

Do not waste my precious rays with this sterile way of thinking and
planning.
Do not communicate with me as if I am a puzzle to be solved or a
code to be cracked.

I am flowing waves of purity.
Only when you approach me as such can we begin to connect.

Bed

My homes are speaking to me this evening.
My chest misses you and cries for your lips again.
My bones are heavy with nostalgia and love.
All the moments of my life that are only stories or memories now
and all the moments of my life that have yet to even begin to occur
are chanting to me, together
through the rainfall.

#chill

Back pop
Fingers click
Heart runs
Feet stick

Toes crack
Breath sits
Eyes read
Floating bits

Thoughts come
Thoughts go
Dreams had
Truths show

Mind circles
Spine slot
Let go
Forget not

March 10, 2013

She just read it. It reminded me of when my middle school students would get called on for popcorn but they totally did not want to be reading. Just fast and straight, get it over with. Anyway, she read it. I remember the preface of the poem. Sobriety. Pain. Healing. All the buzzwords that I held in my repertoire as of the past year and a half or so, easily called upon for therapy sessions. Then, she just read it. I can't recall any lines that stood out to me because I didn't really hear the words. I could just feel the words. I could feel the pain from myself and from her and from anyone else in that living room circle of humans that was dripping out. It collected into a puddle and my soul toweled it up. And I could feel it all. And I cried. I sobbed. Heads stayed still while eyes shifted to peek if my human sadness was real—if this was really happening, a girl sobbing at a cozy community poetry reading? It was happening. A friend scooted over across the circle to be near me, mouthing, "Are you still sober?" Yesyesyes, a million yes's—I nodded with tears flowing. Hands magnetized toward mine and tears magnetized toward those hands as a result. My pain—the pain of self-destruction—came back full force. I could see myself. All those nights, a starry-eyed and wide-mouthed drunk girl stomping in heels and tight skirts down concrete runways between bars. Laughing, always laughing—but never feeling—just numb to the point of laughing. I could see the men touching me, grabbing toward me as I slid off the bar stool, my mouth too drunk to forcefully tell them to back the fuck off. Grazing my wilted body with their thirsty hands, welcomed by my learned insecurity and need for validation from men. I could see night after night after night. Making sure I didn't drive so I could be drunk upon arrival and continue drinking throughout the night. How would I have fun otherwise? Depending on who I was trying to impress that night, my drinks of choice were red wine, PBR, or shots, to put off the vibe that I was fancy, low-maintenance, or could totes handle my liquor (respectfully). Then, I saw the tears. Increasing directly with the length of these choices. My body and soul getting more and more desperate for me to stop this, all of this—what else could they do to try to reach me? Tears from rejection, tears from unwanted accounts of sexual violation, tears from losing control of my body and hurting it, tears from slowly realizing this self-destructive lifestyle was hurting me way more than I could ever pretend it was helping me. Finally, I saw myself in that other college town, taking that last PBR out of the box in some corner of some house at some Halloween party, fake mustache stuck to my face. The sweet crack of it resulting in my drooling, alarmingly resembling Pavlov's dogs and their classical conditioning. That last sip. That last sip when I had had enough. The sip to make me realize I hate this. The same hate that resurfaced this night and demanded to be acknowledged in the presence of others who would understand. I just felt it. And she just read it.

Through The Mirror Of Consciousness I See Myself

What is it about my confidence and my independence that bothers
you so?
What discomforts are reflected to you about yourself when you absorb
the ease with which I walk through my life?
Is it the way I do not confine myself to boxes but, rather, exist as seem-
ingly contradictory things at once that enrages you?
I will not fit the preconceived box you built for me.
I will not surrender into the shallow labels you throw at me.
I will not allow you to run your privilege at me.
Why is this so hard for you to accept?
The way I peacefully exist bothers you so much, the only way you
know how to respond to me is by calling me a name.
Who is the one with the problem here?
It has never been about me. It has always been about you.

Lasting Last Lasts

I have awoken creativity and am coaxing
the baby foxes of it out of their dens
built in the corners of my skin.

Silenced desires of expression longing to be free.
Now I massage dust and knead life into
these parts of me that were shoved down and ignored
even though I could hear my soul howling for these foxes
to run free for years.

Memories romanticized in black and white
forever hold the first and last lesson I will ever know:
always listen to the Earth when she calls to you,
since you are nothing but the Earth.

Made in the USA
Charleston, SC
15 February 2016